Blind Man Holding a Dragon's Tail

Art and Poetry
by
Lawrence Diggs

Blind Man Holding A Dragon's Tail
by Lawrence Diggs
© 2014 by Lawrence Diggs. All rights reserved.

Books may be purchased in quantity and/or special sales by contacting the publisher, Quiet Storm Productions, at P.O. Box 41, Roslyn, South Dakota, USA. You can also make contact at 605-486-4536, or by emailing me@LDiggs.com.

ISBN: 978-0692281581
10 9 8 7 6 5 4 3 2 1
1. Poetry 2. Illustrations
First Edition

The Illustrations

The author created all the illustrations in this book. They are part of a large body of artwork that spans ceramics to 3D animations. His artwork has been sold and exhibited in museums and galleries, on book and music CD covers and sold in art shows and from his websites.

This book has been produced in black and white so to see the works in their full glory they must be experienced in full color. Many of them can be seen at _**www.DiggsArt.com**_. If you are interested in any of the pieces you should contact the author directly.

Dedication

This book is dedicated to Gail "PG" Katagiri. Gail has been a long time fellow traveler on this road and has been there in good times and bad. Thanks and much love.

Acknowledgements

If I have any original ideas, ideas that no one has thought of before, I wouldn't have a clue which they are. Everything I think has come from some suggestion or lesson from someone or something else. I have learned from crickets and crawdads, birds and bacteria to people.

I have benefitted most directly from the Soto Zen Community, especially my friends and family at Soko-ji in San Francisco and Hanya-ji in Tsuruoka, Yamagata Japan. They have been my teachers, supporters and protectors for most of my life.

Sometimes I have learned from successes, but mostly I have learned from lots of dismal, abject mistakes and failures.

I am grateful for all of those who have contributed to who or what I am, whatever that is. I am grateful to those who have made my life full of wonderful people and interesting experiences. I am grateful for those who have allowed me to look through their eyes, sharing their various points of view. They and their points of view have all somehow been absorbed into who I have become.

I am you and you are me and we are all together. Can't remember who told me that.

Special thanks to Gail Katagiri and Betty Sheldon for proof reading and thought checking this manuscript.

Introduction

Much of what we experience or discuss is based on assumptions we make about reality. Funny thing this reality, it is difficult to impossible to know what it is. There have been many deep discussions about the nature of reality, but no tests for it. On the other hand many people avoid struggling with questions about it altogether.

Blind Man Holding a Dragon's Tail is an attempt to engage you in a discussion about the nature of reality. It is a companion to the Interactive Animation Presentations I conduct on various subjects which share the central purpose of helping people find their voice through connecting with others. These presentations are held in private homes, educational institutions, churches, business training sessions and conventions.

Blind Man Holding a Dragon's Tail raises many questions. I invite you to use it as a catalyst to engage in discussions. Use it to get others to share their points of view with you, allowing you to refine and give greater depth to your own. Use it as a launch pad to explore other realities. Welcome aboard.

Most of the poems in this book were written in the "Dyslexic-senile" style to accommodate my idiosyncrasies.

You can contact me about my Interactive Animation Presentations at 605 486 4536 or by email at: me@ldiggs.com. You can also visit my websites at www.DiggsArt.com or www.LDiggs.com to find out other things I am doing or join my email list and DiggsWorld community.

Table of Contents

Blind Man Holding a Dragon's Tail 1
Standing at the Station 3
Scenes from the Window of a Train 5
The Shadow is Mu 7
Kage Wa Mu 9
Change 10
First Instruction to the Magi 13
Winning 14
Dia Del Morte 17
Mostly Nothing 19
Illusions 21
What is reality? 23
Finely Focused Reality 24
Freewill Revisited 27
Terminal Effect 28
Event Horizon 31
Lying eyes 32
Reality is Too Big for the Mind 33
Frames 34
The Transducers 37
Consciousness is a Chemical Reaction 39
The Calm Must Come From Within 41
Here We Be 43
Busy Doing What Don't Need Done 45
The One Drop Rule 47
Illumination 48
Struggle 49
Life's Contradiction 51
Infinity 52
The Sum of All Numbers 53
Just an Illusion 55
A Tricky Thing 57
Location, Location, Time 59
Blindness 61

Cause and Effect Dilemma 63
Fixing My Coordinates 65
Reality's Foundation 67
Newton's Third Law 69
Ohm's Law 71
The Universe is Perfect 73
Practicing Patience 75
If You Ain't At Eye Level You Ain't 77
Morphing 79
Memory Can be Overrated 80
Fate 83
Phantom Pain 85
The Multiverses 87
Reality & Desire 89
A Vortex 91
Shifting Internal Reality 93
All We Really Want is Drama 95
About the Author 96
Epilogue 97
Suggested Reading 98

Blind Man Holding a Dragon's Tail

We cannot see
We cannot see
It's hard to admit but
We cannot see

But being blind
We reach
With the mind
Grasping for reality

Something comes
Within our grasp
We grab
And pronounce it reality

How can a
Blind man know
He is holding
The tail of a dragon?

Standing at the Station

Standing at the station
All the trains, same destination

Some Express
Some limited
Some local

Leaving early
Leaving later

Some over the mountain
Some through the tunnel
Some over the plains

Some fancy
Some plain

Some with comforts
Some with pain

Standing at the station
All the trains, same destination

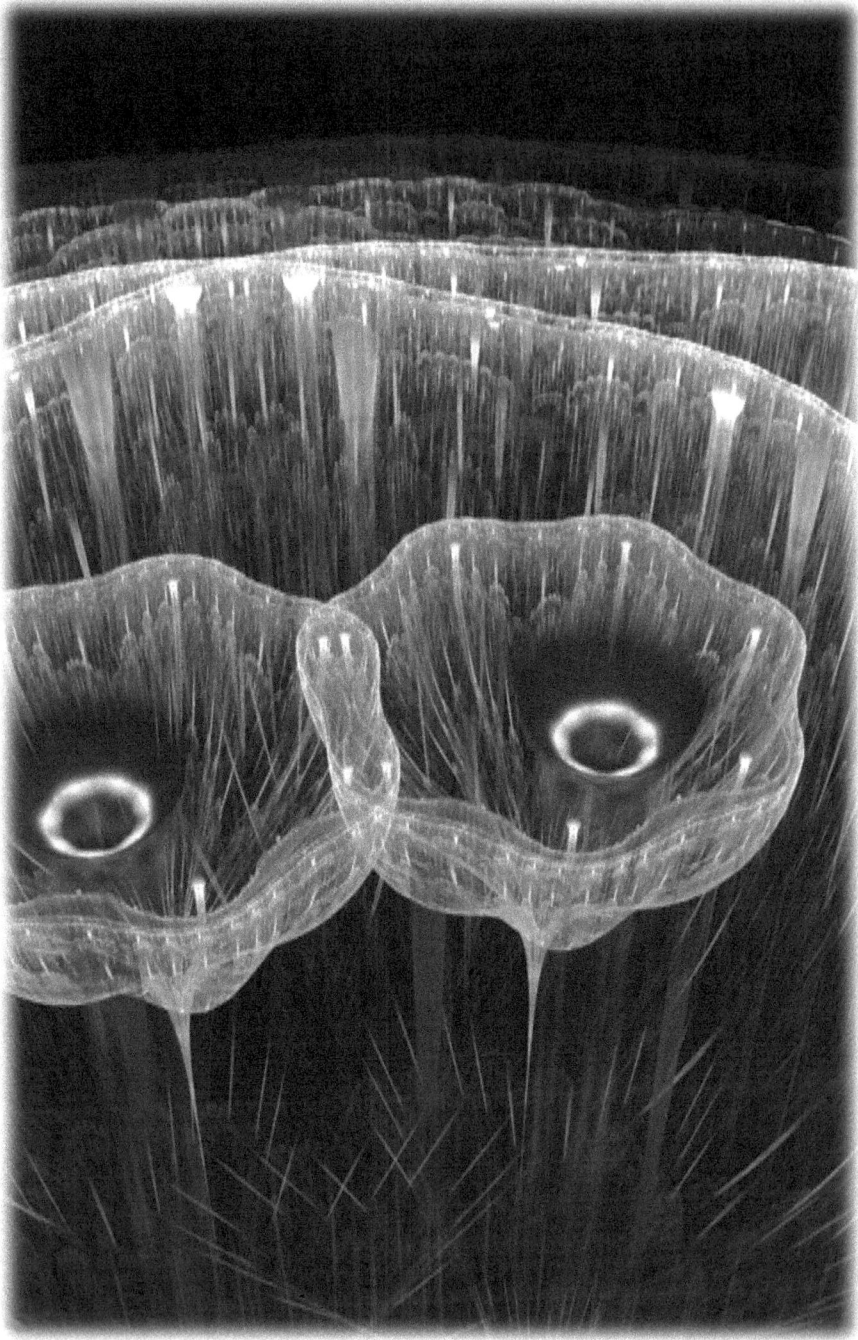

Scenes from the Window of a Train

Women dreaming of poets
but marrying drill sergeants

Money is only paper

A body is a person package

Life results in death

Possessions imprison

White space speaks

There are worse professions than prostitution

We are at war with ourselves

The senses are reality filters

The weakness of men is the façade of strength
The strength of women is the façade of weakness

Things are not as they seem

Most of our efforts are spent trying to avoid the inevitable

Relationships have fine print and unstated expectations

Memory is overrated

I missed my stop

The Shadow is Mu

The Shadow is Mu

A colorless transparent thing
An odorless thing
A tasteless thing
The Shadow is mu

A nameless thing
An egoless thing
A blameless thing
The Shadow is mu

A perpetually moving thing
A formless thing
An effortlessly moving thing
The Shadow is mu

A form that takes nothing
A form that gives nothing
A form that exist
Yet does not exist
The Shadow is mu

Kage Wa Mu

Kage wa mu

Mushooku no mono
Mushuu no mono
Mumi no mono
Kage wa mu

Mumei no mono
Muchi no mono
Muzai no mono
Kage wa mu

Itsumo kawaruno katachi
Katachi ga nai no katachi
Muzosa ni ugoku no katachi
Kage wa mu

Nanimo toranai no katachi
Nanimo agenai no katachi
Iru kedo inai no katachi
Kage wa mu

Change

Some folks say they see no change
They must have never been on the range
Looking up they could notice
They are under a sky of change

Some folks say they want no change
To rearrange is to misarrange
Looking up they could notice
The creator paints a sky of change

Some folks say they need no change
They need the same folks holding the reins
Looking up they could notice
From horizon to horizon, change

The universe is in a state of flux
Nothing is static in its construct
And all that's within it complies

If we resist modification, alteration, and variation
How do we accomplish adaptation?
From where do we get our supplies?

Innovation, diversification and transformation
Are all part of a transmutation
Happening before our eyes

Change is happening on both sides of our eyes
It happens without our compromise

We can
Agonize, apologize, compartmentalize,
Containerize, conventionalize, criticize, crystallize
Centralize, criminalize, categorize,
Disguise, Dramatize, eulogize, evangelize
Fanaticize, fictionalize, finalize, formalize, fossilize, franchise,
Gelatinize, glamorize, homogenize,
Hypnotize, harmonize, idealize, idolize, immobilize, immortalize,
Immunize, intellectualize, legitimize, lionize, localize
Militarize, memorialize, memorize, moralize,
methodize, monopolize
Narcotize, nationalize, neutralize,
Ostracize, organize
Paralyze, pasteurize, philosophize, politicize, privatize,
Rationalize, regularize, ritualize, robotize, romanticize, routinize
Sanitize, scandalize, scrutinize, serialize, sermonize, soliloquize,
Stabilize, sterilize, supervise, systematize
Traditionalize, tranquilize, tyrannize,
Unionize, unitize
Westernize, weatherize

But life is like Dakota skies
And no one denies
There is always change in Dakota skies

First Instruction to the Magi

Keep your eyes on the horizon
All things must pass
All that you are meant to see, you shall see
And all that you have seen you shall see again
Your designs cannot direct your destiny
You control nothing here
Your desires and deeds do not direct the universe
You cannot make it better
You cannot make it worse
The universe is perfect
The All seeing   All knowing   Almighty Creator
Does not make mistakes

Winning

I had a patient once
On the psyche ward
In a long term care facility

He had reduced his life's goal
To one mission statement

No matter what was said to him
His response was
I want to win

He repeated this one phrase
All day
Over and over

One day I asked him
What do you want to win?
He paused for a moment
Chuckled and replied
I want to win

It occurred to me that
The only difference
Between him
And many of us is
He was institutionalized

We are in it
To win it
But win what?

Here we sit
On this speck of spit
In a vast universe
Of time and space
Spinnin' and winnin'
Winnin' what?

Like a race horse runnin'
With no sense of the senselessness
Of the circle
We want to get ahead
Get ahead of what?
Of whom?
To what end?
We just want to win

We want to win certificates
We want to win trophies
We want to win medals
We want to win praise
We want to win braggin' rights

We risk life and limb   to win
We destroy each other   to win
We sacrifice valuable relationships   to win

We just want to win
But to what end?

Is earth
The universe's psyche ward
For those who
Want to win?

Dia Del Morte

On our day of death
With our last breath
We abort
Our prison and our fort
Our substance separates
From our sack

All our woulda-coulda-shoulda's
Are distanced
Abandoned to defend
For themselves

All our to-dos and to-don'ts
Disappear from
Our in and out boxes
And shelves

Our me's
Become our histories
Our we's that were
Our hurries and worries
Are reduced to ripples
In the redundancies
Of cause and effect

And this may be
As close to immortality
As we may ever get

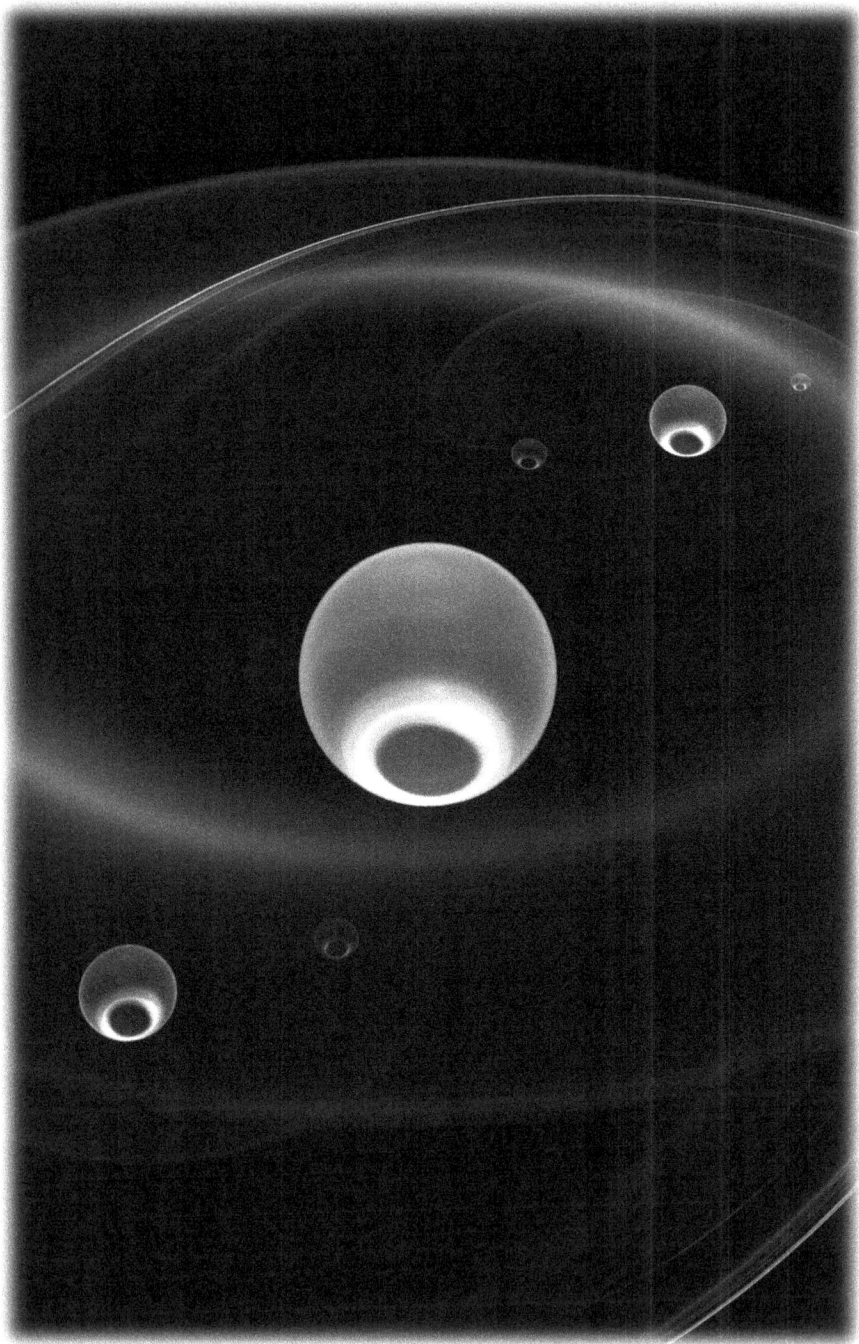

Mostly Nothing

Between the protons, electrons and neutrons
Mostly nothing

Between the atoms
Mostly nothing

Between the elements
Mostly nothing

Between the molecules
Mostly nothing

Between things
Mostly no-things

Between planets
Mostly no-things

Between stars
Mostly nothing

Between galaxies
Mostly nothing

The universe as we perceive it
Mostly nothing

Reality as we can grasp it
Mostly nothing

Is existence a false paradigm?

Illusions

Memories of the past
Visions of the future
Create the view of the present

The Heisenberg Principle

It seems that reality
Is not cognitively perceivable
By the human mind

The present is the hypothetical place
Between the past and the future

We move from the future to the past
On the supposition that we are
Experiencing the present

If the past and future
Are cognitive creations
And the present,
If it exists at all
So fleeting that it is
Imperceptible to the human mind
What then is reality?
How can it be distilled from illusion?

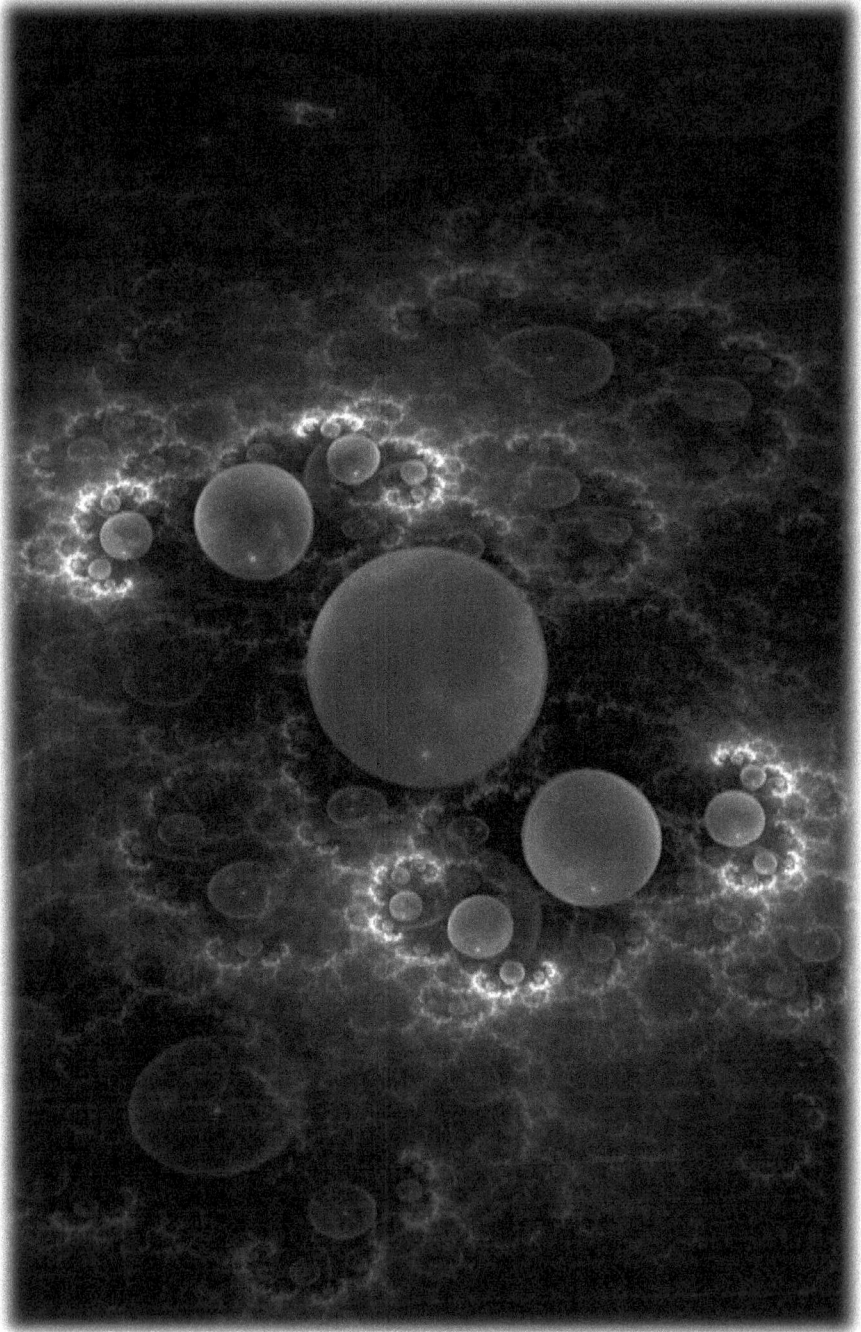

What is reality?

How do we fix our coordinates
In an omni-directional universe?
How do we know where we have been
Or where we are going?
What thing is moving?
What thing is still?

Stars
Appearing to be fixed
Are on closer observation
Speeding through space

Mountains
Appearing to be immovable
Are on closer observation
Rising and falling
Expanding and contracting
Rotating and orbiting with the earth

Stones and other things
Appearing to be at rest
Are on closer observation
Vibrating furiously
Shifting continuously
Morphing

Finely Focused Reality

The finely focused photos
We snap with our minds
Lead us to believe we can know
The dynamic whole
By observing the static parts

We're surprised and bewildered
When the pieces of the puzzle
Fail to fit

We're dumbfounded
When our discontiguous snippets
Fail to fit some organic theory of
Everything

How could they
When what we have seen,
Compared to what there is
Amounts to
Nothing?

Our dependency on focus
Renders us blind

While we focus
On any minutia
The rest of reality
Goes about its business
Leaving us to believe
We have perceived
Something

We can never really understand anything

So much is hidden behind
The veil of our inadequate eyes

So much is out of focus

While we focus on one thing
The limits of our brain render us
Oblivious to the rest of reality

Freewill Revisited

I cannot say whether
Or not I believe in freewill
Because I cannot determine
What it is

What can be the meaning of freewill
When reality itself is in question?

Terminal Effect

The movement of a thing
Itself a transitional effect of
The Prime Mover
Becomes the cause of
A cascading set of effects
Which themselves become
Cascading causes of
Cascading effects in
Geometric progression
Acting on each other

What then is the terminal effect of any cause?

Can there be a terminal effect?

How can there be a terminal effect?

How can we calculate the terminal effect?

Is it possible to affect the effect?

Looking through the frame of cause and effect
What does freewill look like?
Assuming a Prime Mover
All causes and effects
Are extensions of the prime movement
It is assumed that nothing exists outside of this
What then does freewill look like through this frame?

Without knowledge of the terminal effect
How can we plot our path?
Without knowledge of the terminal effect

How can we know the consequences of our actions?
Without knowledge of the terminal effect
How can we elect, direct and or detect the effect of our affect?

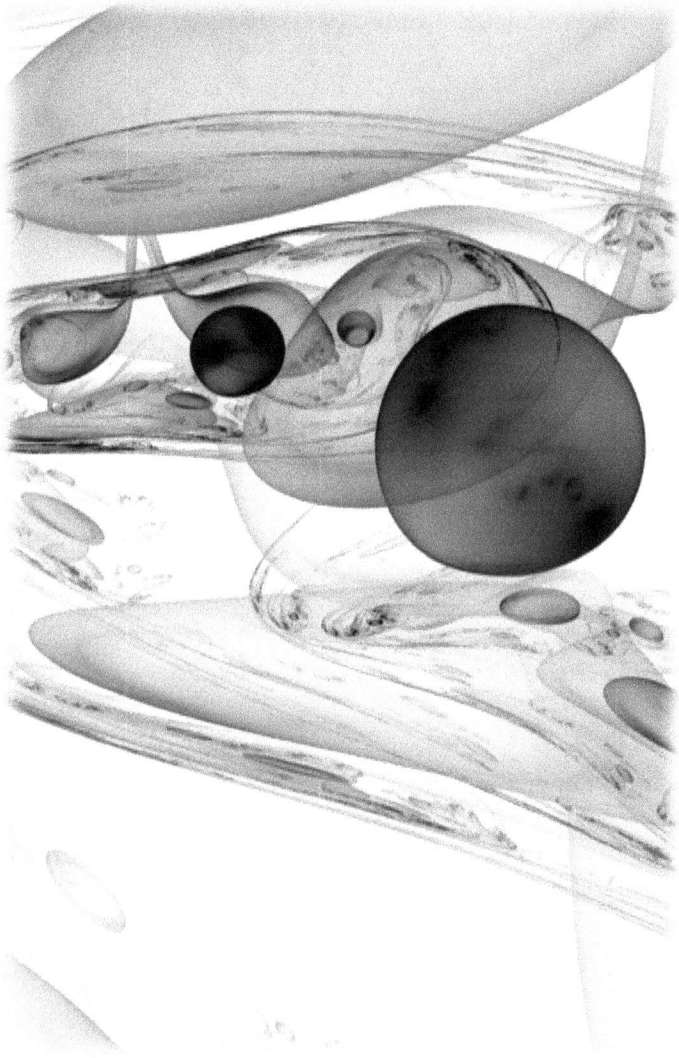

Event Horizon

Every moment we cross some event horizon
Those invisible lines over which
When crossed
An event has happened
Though it has not yet happened

At this very moment
Some subtle line has been crossed
Some subtle force has pivoted
Some wind has shifted
Some timing adjusted
Lining you up
With some unseen
Unimaginable
Inescapable
Event

When requisite causes converge
At the event horizon
Freewill is mute,
Resistance futile.
The affect
Is already
In full effect

Lying eyes

The sky we see is
The sky as it was

The sun we see is the sun
As it was 12 minutes before

The stars we see are
The stars as they were
Many years ago

The dynamic universe we live in
Has changed by the time we
Make a thought of it

The observer is always separated
From the observed by time
So the present cannot be observed

How then can we experience the present?

Reality is Too Big for the Mind

The senses suck
In more sensations
Than the mind
Can make sense of

But the mind does not like
The abyss of not knowing

So the mind gorges on data
Until it chokes and vomits
Illusions

A satisfied mind
Sleeping in its own vomit

Frames

All of what we know
Is framed by the unknown

What is
Is framed by
What is not

It is the frame
That defines what we see
More than what is seen

Nothing can be seen
Without a frame

Everything is experienced
Through and within a frame

What is experienced
Is framed
By what has not been experienced

"Culture"
Is only a Frame

Sound
Is framed by silence

Light is framed
By darkness and shadows

Beliefs
Are framed by disbelief

Differences
Are framed by similarities

Consciousness
Is framed by unconsciousness

The familiar
Is framed by the strange

The present
Is framed by imagined time

The imagined
Is framed by the unimagined

Can
Is framed by can't
Is framed by can

Nothing is infinite
Only nothing is unframed

What then is reality?
It's a mere veneer
Manufactured by the mind
From materials of its own making
In the process of making meaning
From patterns seen through frames

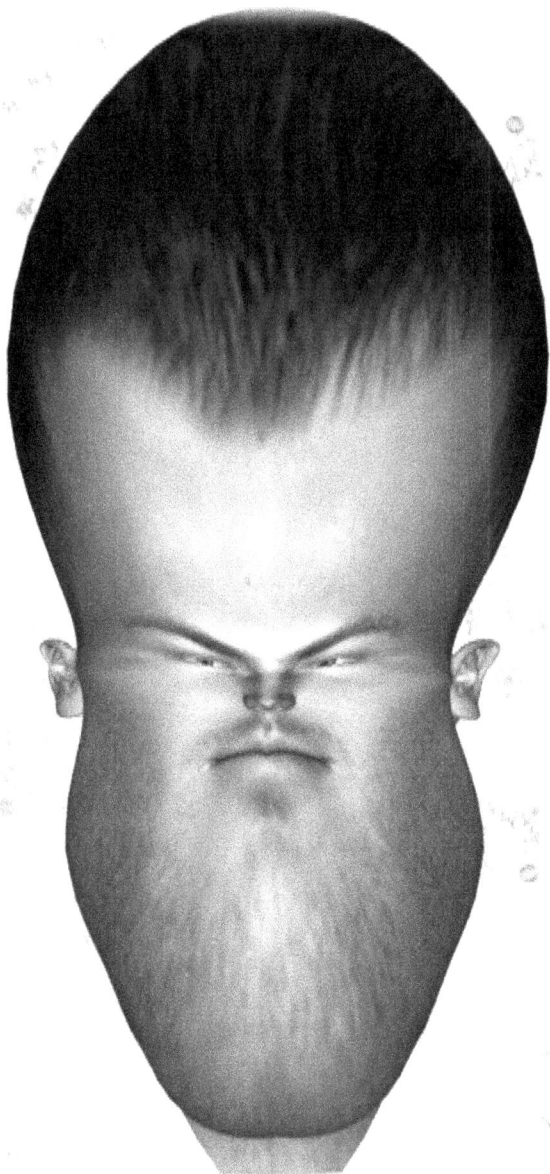

The Transducers

The eyes are limited to a narrow band of light energy
All else appears as darkness

The ear cannot hear out of its range
All else is silence

The nose can only perceive
Selected chemicals in a volatile state
All else is odorless

The tongue can only detect 5 tastes
And must coordinate with the nose to create
The experience of taste
All else is tasteless

The nerves that pick up pressure and temperature
Can only sense that which stimulates them in a certain fashion
All else does not exist

The feeling transducers send
Signals based on relative
And contrasting changes in the
Immediate environment
All else is non-existent

So, are these transducers transmitting reality
Or filtering it
And thus creating illusion?

What facsimile of reality can
The mind create
With such faulty data?

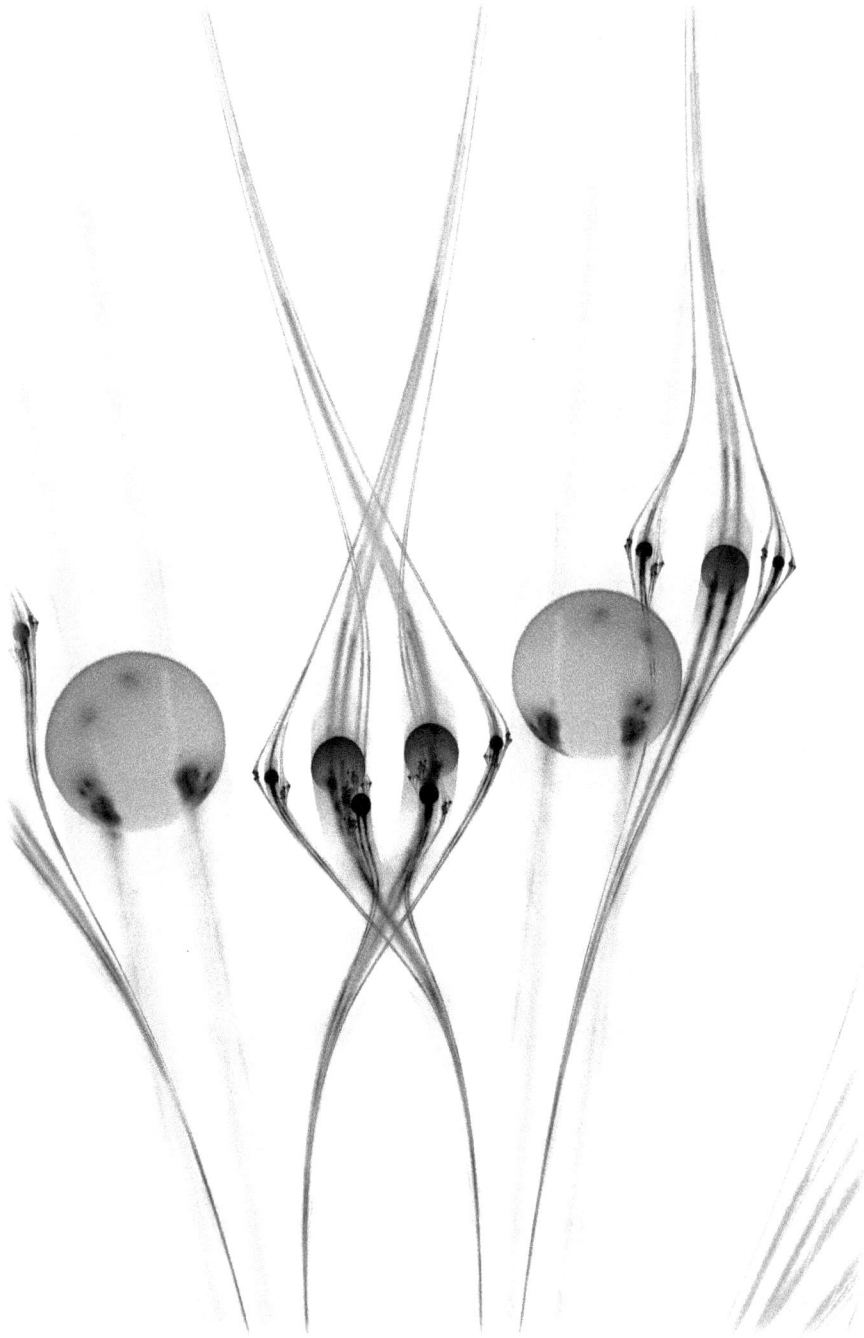

Consciousness is a Chemical Reaction

There are no random Numbers
There are no straight lines
There are no accidents or blunders
There's no such thing as time

There's only a creator
And some reactions in our brains
None of us are conductors
Only riders on this train

The Calm Must Come From Within

There will always be a storm outside
And there may be no place to hide
The calm then
Must Come from within

There will always be those who rattle your cage
Eager to share their contagious rage
The calm then
Must Come from within

There will always be more to get
There are always reasons to fret
The calm then
Must Come from within

There is a space, to escape the race
And that place is your inner space
The calm then
Will come from within

Here We Be

Here we be
Cast adrift
Between our
Ought to bees
Want to bees
Need to bees
And inadequacies

Here we be
Floating frantically
Between
Who we be
And who we hope to be
Here we be
And that's
What keeps us buzzin'

Busy Doing What Don't Need Done

Goin' Goin'
Comin' comin'
Never time 'cause I'm under the gun
Busy doin' what don't need done

Buyin' buyin'
Sellin' sellin'
Makin' money when I don't need none
To do more things that don't need done

Messin' Messin'
Stressin' stressin'
Creatin' a life that ain't much fun
'Cause I'm doin' things that don't need done

Graspin' graspin'
Gaspin' gaspin'
And in the end what have I won
By doin' things that don't need done?

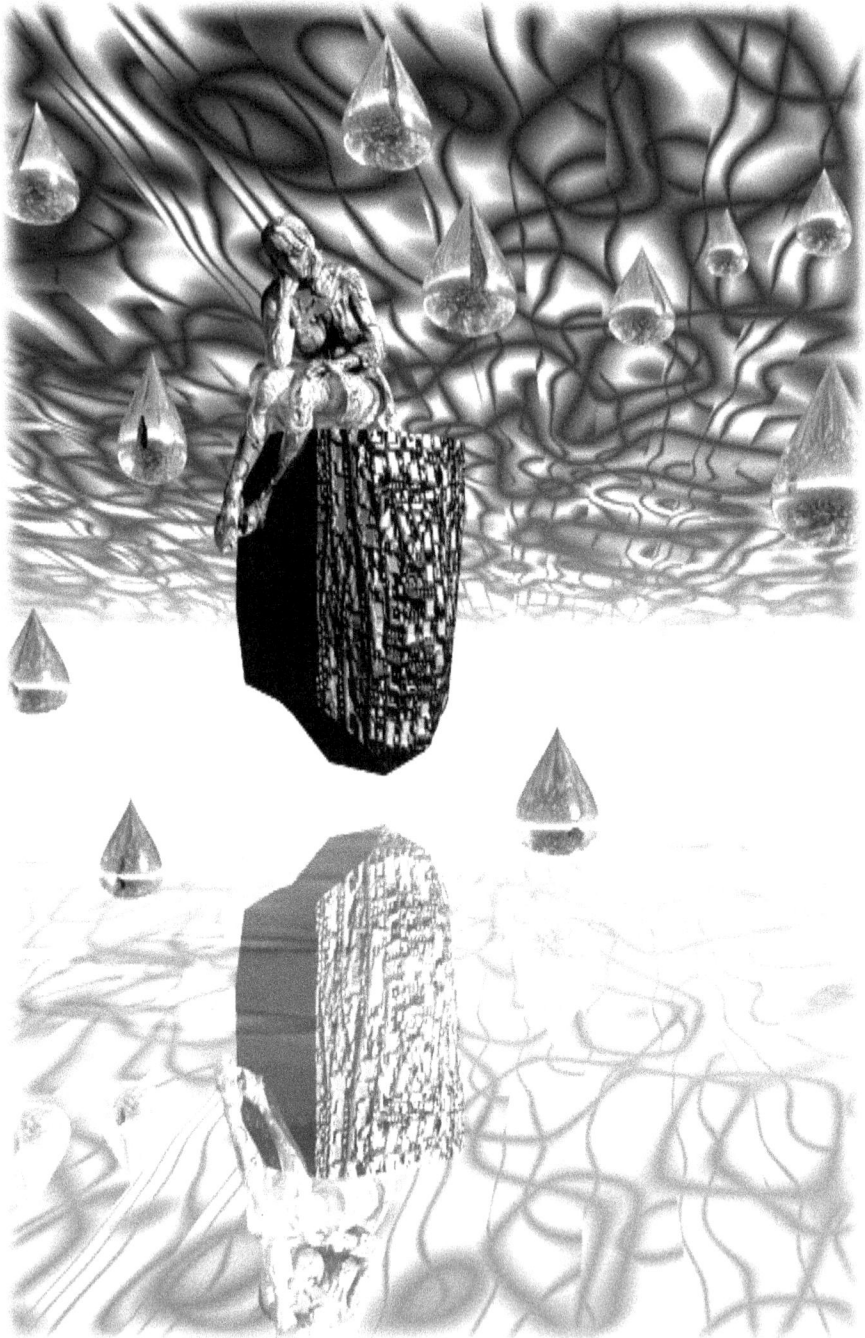

The One Drop Rule

How do we find a raindrop
After it falls to the sea?
Where does it go?
What is its shape?
What does it become?
Does it still exist?

Illumination

Subjects can be hidden as well
By an excess of light
As they can by a lack of it

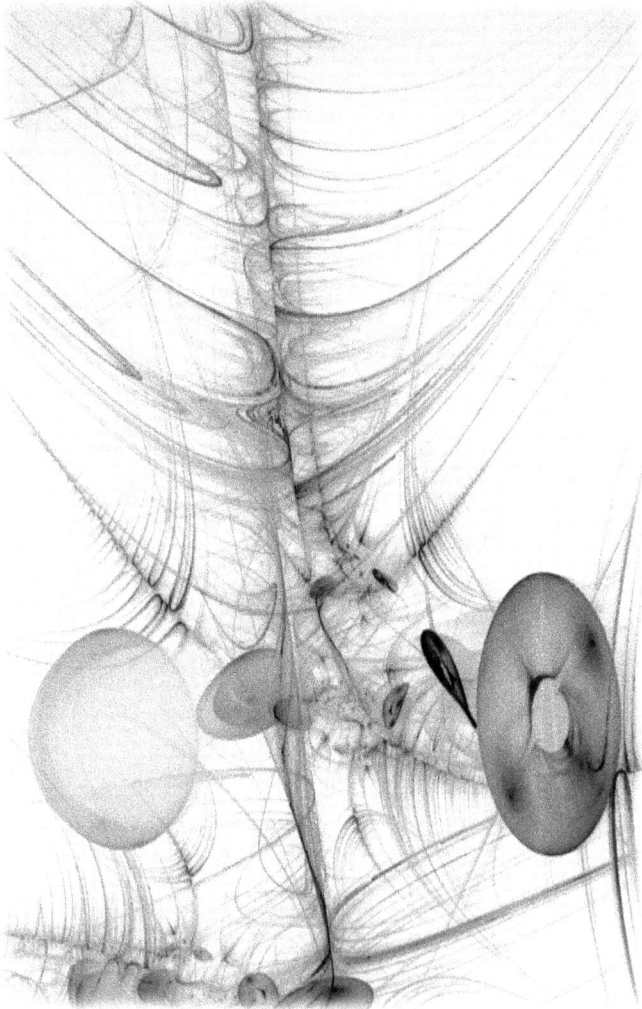

Struggle

The sea is stormy and rocks all around
But as of yet we have not run aground
Or have we?

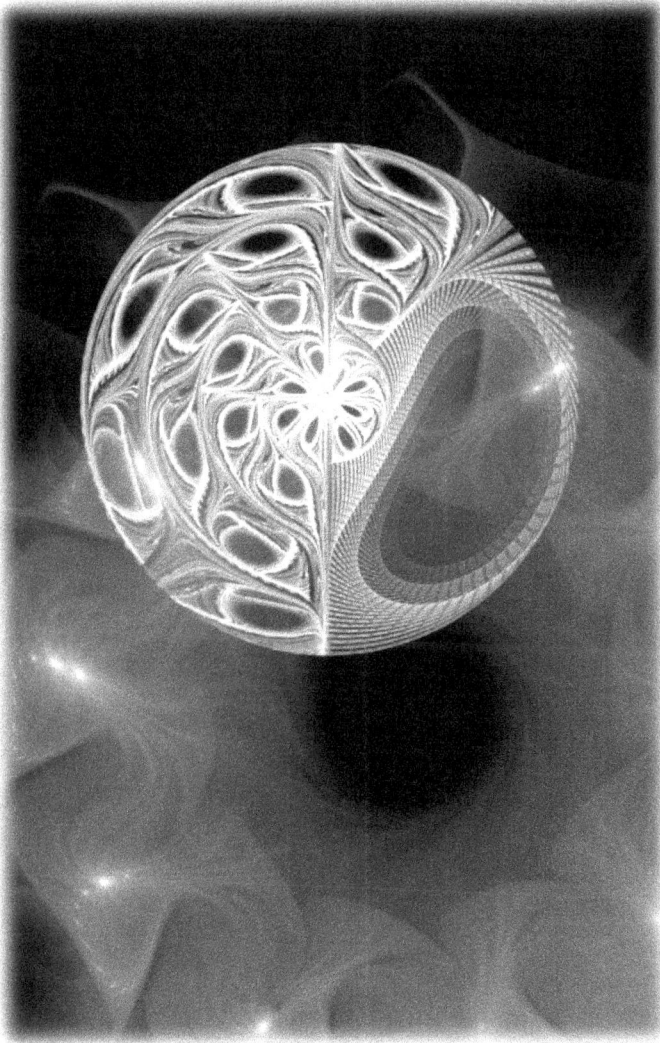

Life's Contradiction

If we managed to isolate ourselves
From all that could kill us
Then could we have managed
To kill ourselves?

Infinity

Infinity is a difficult concept to grasp
Because of our illusion of
Discrete entities
And linear time
What lies just beyond
Is beyond
Our perception?

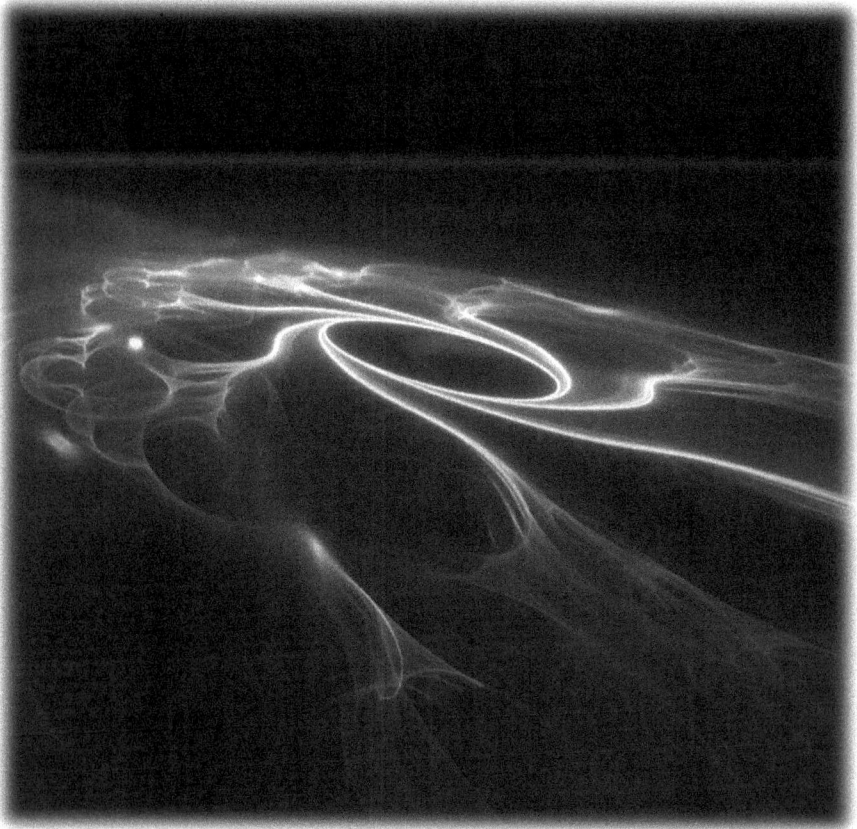

The Sum of All Numbers

A fleeting moment in time and space
Inhale, exhale, villain, hero
The sum of all numbers is zero

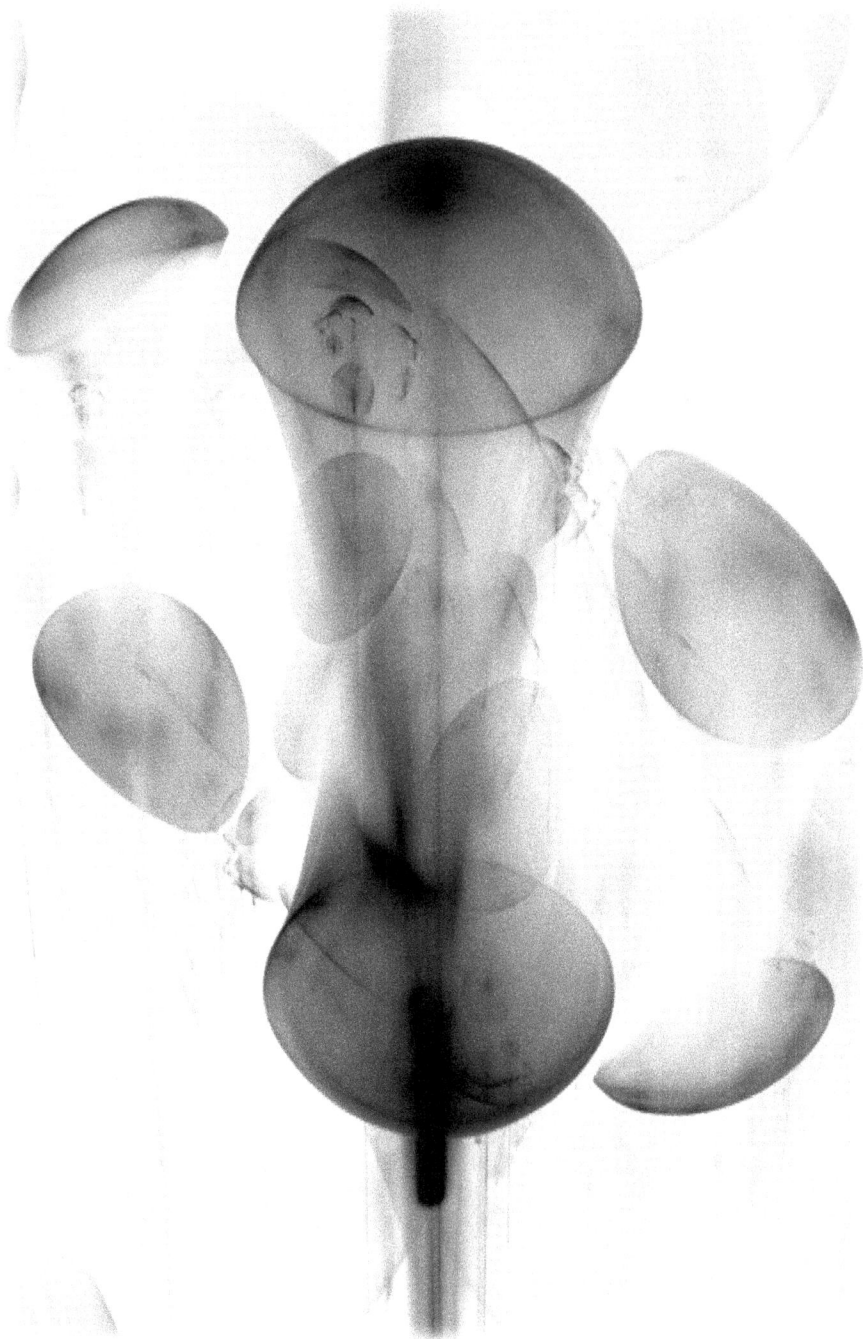

Just an Illusion

I am just an illusion

If I seem tall it is because
I am standing on the shoulders of giants

If I seem small it is because
I am standing next to giants

A Tricky Thing

Reality can be a tricky thing
Mere observation of a thing
Causes it to change
While you are working on answers
The questions change
Working on answers
Causes the questions to change
How can we catch smoke
With chopsticks?

Location, Location, Time

Trees growing on a hill
Thrive until there is drought
Trees growing near a slough
Thrive until there is flooding
How do we plan for an uncertain future
When the present is unknowable
And the past unknown?
What is the meaning of free will
When the multi-effects
Any action causes
Is unknowable?

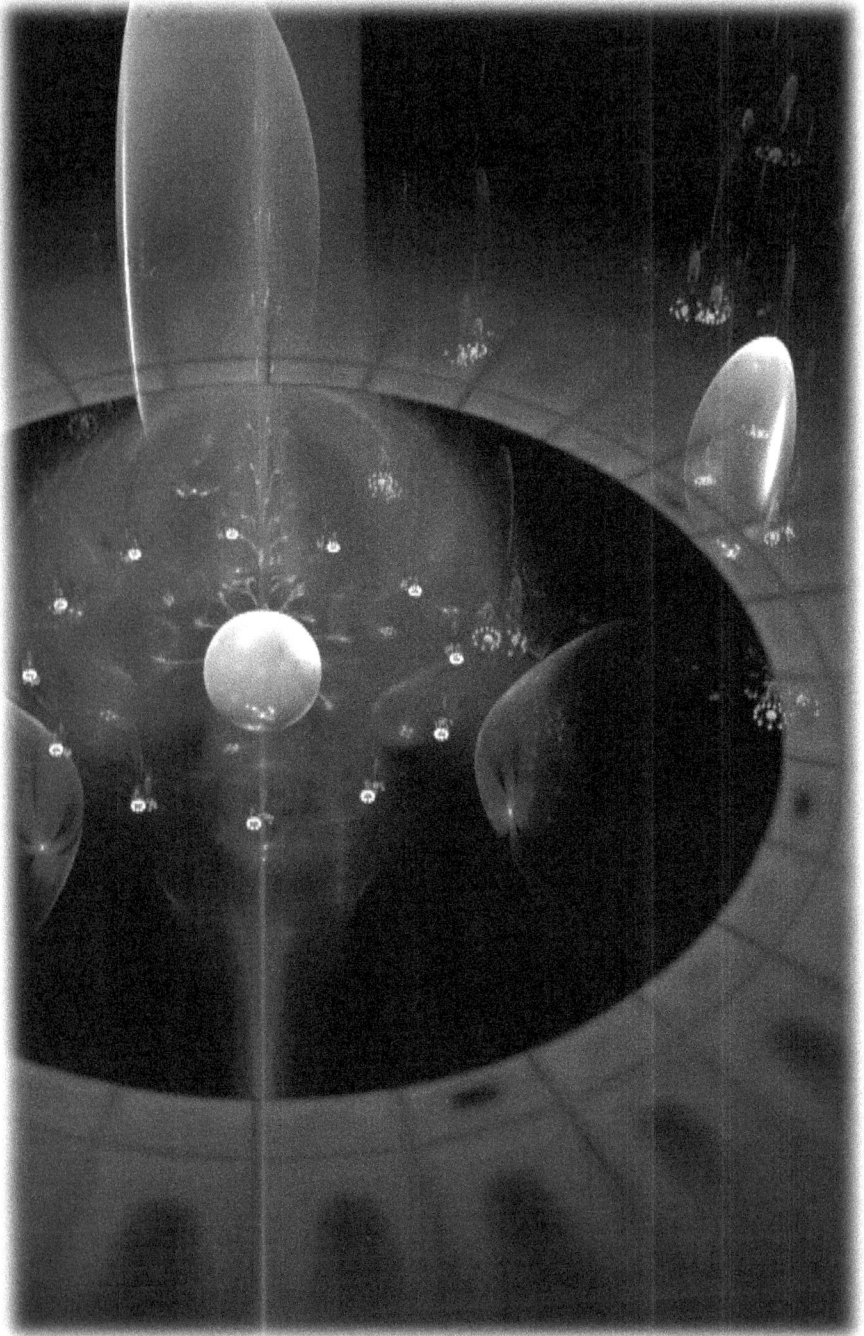

Blindness

There is no chaos, only incomprehensible order

There are no random numbers,
Only our inability to see patterns

There is no chaos
Only our inability to see patterns

There is no darkness
Only our inability to see
Outside of a narrow spectrum

We are blinded
By the illusion that we can see

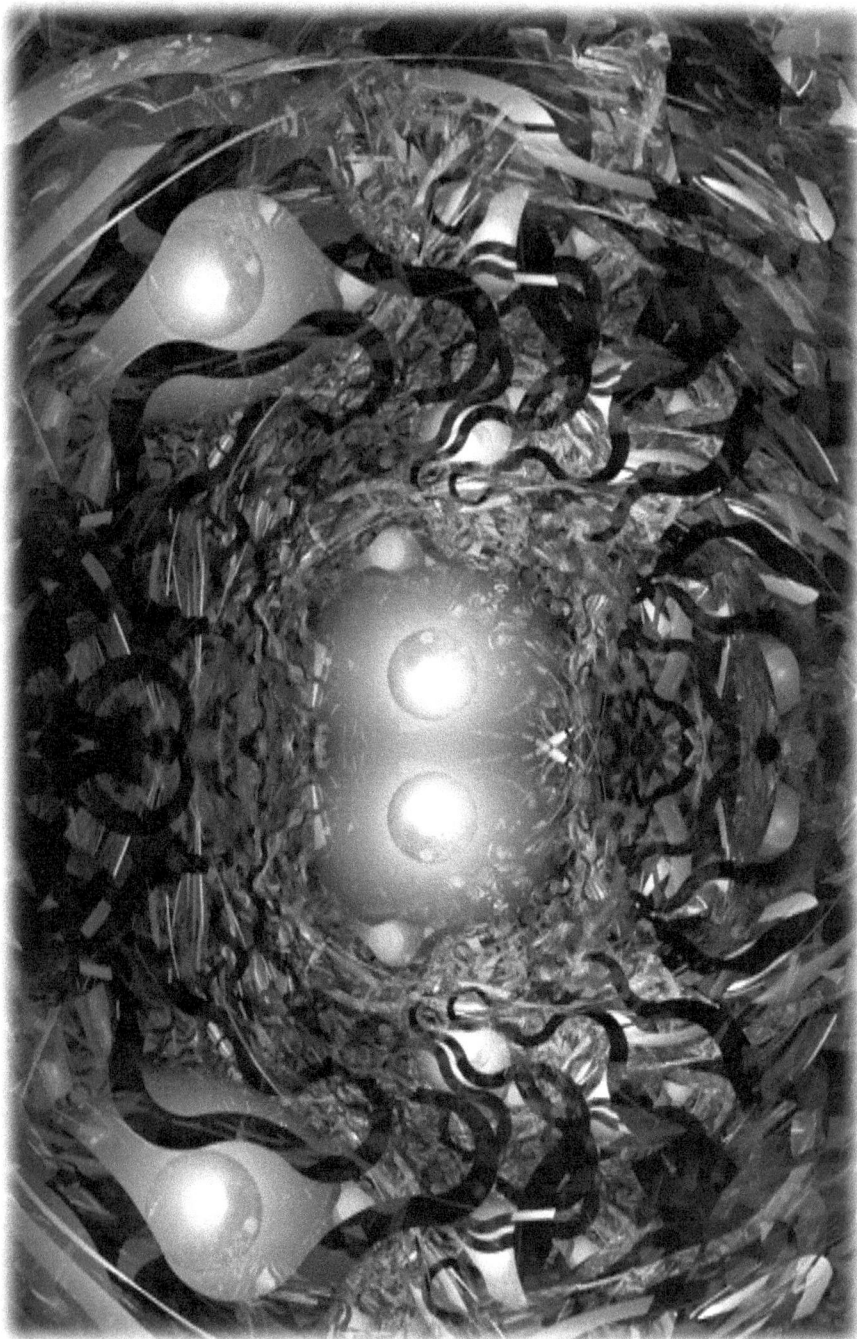

Cause and Effect Dilemma

What is the terminal effect of the prime movement?
When every cause becomes an effect
And every effect a cause
In an endless loop
When every cause and effect
Causes ripples
Of causes and effects
Each influencing and being influenced
By all the other ripples
Of causes and effects
What will be the terminal effect of the prime movement?
What part will my causes and effects play?
Am I a cause
Or an effect?
Am I relevant?

Fixing My Coordinates

I seem to be positioned somewhere between
The primary cause and the terminal effect

Not knowing the position of either
Is it possible to know
Where I am
Or the point of my existence?

That acknowledged
I am just as capable
As everyone else
Of making use of
Reality placebos

Reality's Foundation

What is the sustained basis
Upon which our mutual reality rests?
On what is it that we can all agree?
Where do our realities diverge?
Where do they converge?
How do we collect
Connect and coordinate
All of our realities
Into a shared reality
That we may visit
On a vacation from
Our mundane
And solitary
Madness?

Newton's Third Law

If for every action
There is an equal and opposite reaction
What is the meaning of energy?
If for every action
There is an equal and opposite reaction
What is the meaning of effort?

Ohm's Law

V=IxR
There is no voltage without resistance
Why not appreciate
The role resistance plays
In creating the voltage
In our lives?

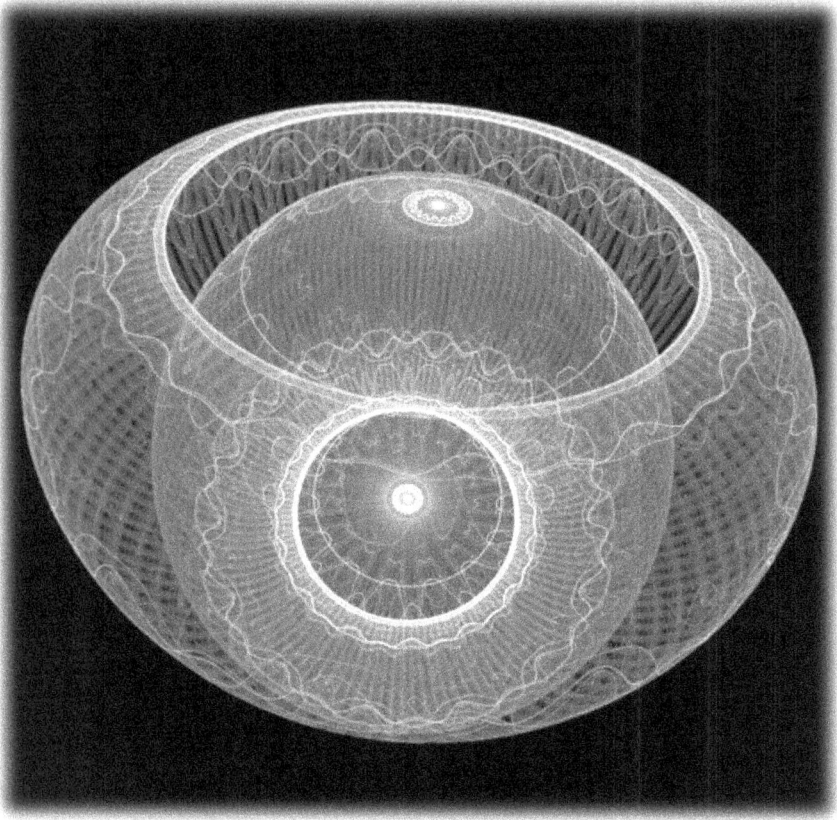

The Universe is Perfect

The universe is perfect
The creator
Does not make mistakes
Everything is in its place
In the universe
There are no extra pieces
Things may not be going
According to our plan
But somehow
They seem to be
Going according to
THE Plan

Practicing Patience

Time is a universal lever
Change a small thing
A small amount
And watch it grow
To a big thing

But when to work?
When to wait?

A stitch in time saves nine
But haste makes waste

When is taking the initiative
Just hubris?

When is practicing patience
Just procrastination?

If You Ain't At Eye Level You Ain't

If you ain't at eye level you ain't
I won't look up 'cause you think you're a saint
I won't look down while pretending you're quaint
You can pitch a fit and threaten to hit
You can fall on the floor and faint
But the right place to be is the same level as me
If you ain't at eye level you ain't

Morphing

At what point does a changed thing cease to be the thing?

When does black, on its way to being white, not be either?
When does large, on its way to being small, lose its grandeur?
When does bad, on its way to being good, become acceptable?
When does up, on its way down, lose its position?
When does hard, on its way to being soft, lose its feeling?

Are there names for all of the in-between states?

Memory Can be Overrated

The ability to re-member
Or more accurately
Re-create Some reality
Is overrated

A "real" event
Itself constructed of
A mere mist of what existed
Is re-membered
With many missing members

Each re-membrance
Becomes an original
Unique event
As the mind throws putty
Between the cracks
To fill the gaps
Where the re-membered members
Fail to fit

Sometimes there's not enough putty,
But the imagination has
An unlimited supply of duct tape
And members of other realities
From which new memories
Can be re-membered

When there are
No members available
The mind can re-member reality
From self constructed members and
Mount it on a scaffolding of
How we want it to be

Who needs a memory
When you have creativity?
The Easter eggs you hide
Can provide a lifetime
Of discovery
If you lack memory

You meet so many new nice people
Who pretend they know you so well

Some people are victimized
By a good memory
The memories re-play nonstop
Maddening the victim

They can't forget
They can't forget small slights
They can't forget dirty looks
They can't forget debts
They can't forget their mistakes
Or the mistakes of others

Their minds are so cluttered
With the memories of life's minutia that
Meaning is missing

They become imprisoned in the past
Unable to experience the present

They never meet new people
Or experience new realities

Memory is so overrated

Fate

Soon the final fate will befall us all
Now we can stand
Some of us tall
But we're riding a conveyor belt
With no clue of the fall
We can't say where or when
We'll get the call
But the final fate will befall us all

Phantom Pain

Some problems are like a phantom itch
At the end of an amputated limb

It shouldn't be there but it is

Never mind that the itching limb
On which the illusion is based
Does not exist
The maddening itch persists

You can clearly see
And readily agree
That it should not be
But still it bothers

Rational thought did not bring it
Rational thought cannot take it
It is not emotional
It is not rational
It just sits there
Ill defined
In a place that does not exist

It may be all in your head
But it cannot be found there either

The uninitiated
Are unimpressed
And unsympathetic

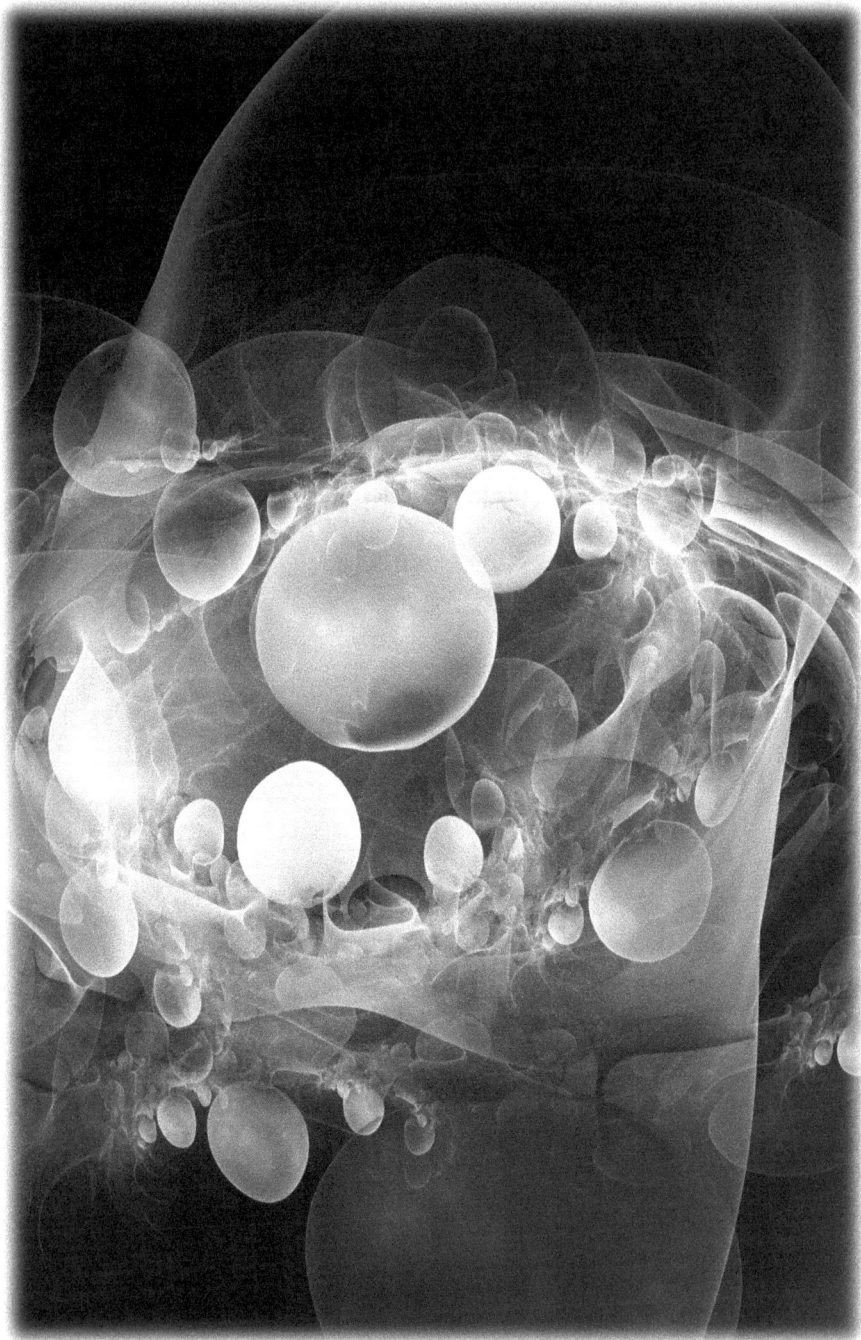

The Multiverses

There seems to be some question
In some quarters
As to whether there is one universe
All inclusive

Or whether there are many universes
Co-existing, perhaps in parallel
Occupying the same space and time
All inclusive

Could it be that each of us exist
In our own universal bubble?
Could it be that relationships
Are made by those bubbles joining
Like soap bubbles in a pan?

Could it be that loneliness
Is floating alone in your own bubble?

Are there unseen
Unknown
Bubble barriers?
Are there forces that pull bubbles together?
Are there universal surfactants
Acting on our bubbles?
How do we join bubbles?

Reality & Desire

What I want is shaped by
What I can imagine and think is possible
What I feel determines
What is real
We are feeling beings that think
Not thinking beings that feel

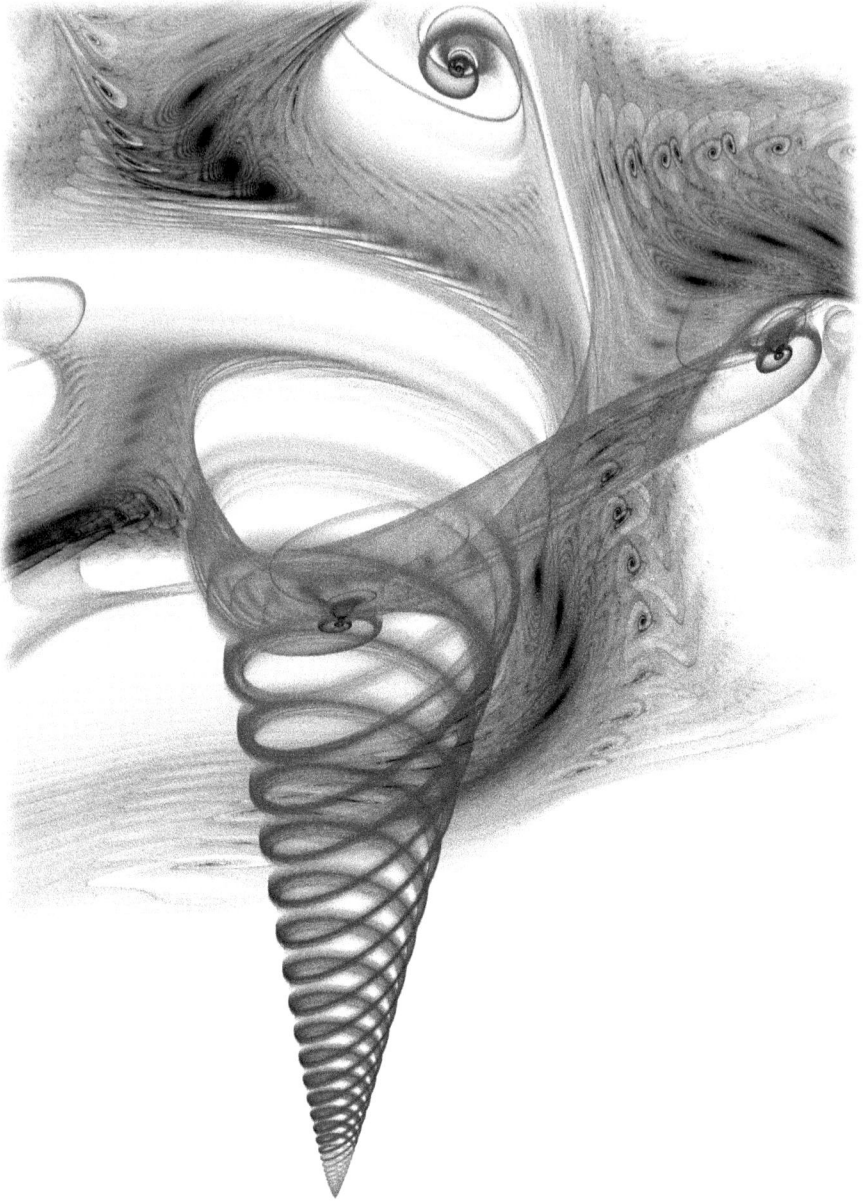

A Vortex

A Vortex
A tornado
A whirlwind
A whirlpool
A black hole

A Vortex
Some irresistible
Invisible force
Sucking us over
The next event horizon

Some action at a distance

Some internal,
Unknown need
That overrides
Our rational thought
Neutralizes our will power
Blinds us to
True self interest

A diabetic
A doughnut

A man
A woman

A gambler
A casino

A smoker
Tobacco

A drunkard
A drink

A sinner
A sin

Good has a better product
But bad has a better marketing department

Shifting Internal Reality

It is easier to think of abstinence
After indulgence

It is easier to think of exercise
After rest

It is easier to think of fasting
After eating

It is easier to think of peace
During war

It is easier to think of saving
After spending

It is easier to think of silence
While its noisy

All We Really Want is Drama

Let us rid ourselves of the thinker
Before he begins to tinker
And rob us of all our pollution

We love to flop in this human slop
We don't need no stinking solutions

Real solutions will bring us trauma
And all we really want is drama

About the Author

Lawrence Diggs Left San Francisco to become a resident of Roslyn, South Dakota, where he has lived for over 25 years.

He has hosted radio and television shows in major markets in the United States, Europe and Asia. He has written and published six books and is a regular columnist for the Aberdeen American News.

Lawrence Diggs is a South Dakota Humanities Scholar who writes and performs music and poetry in English and Japanese. He makes presentations on topics ranging from food and culture to human perception, gender issues, and the imaginary lines of "race".

In addition to literary arts, he currently works in live performance, musical composition, photography, 3D digital painting and animation, microbial fiber and ceramics.

He founded and was the curator of the International Vinegar Museum. He is the author of a textbook, and subsequently internationally known as an expert, on the production, marketing and use of vinegar. He has served as president and vice president of the South Dakota Specialty Producers Association. He serves on the board of directors of the South Dakota State Poetry Society.

In Japan he organized the Shonai Jazz Festival. He helped start and served two terms as vice president of the Shonai International Youth Festival.

In Burkina Faso he set up the first emergency medical response system, filled in as a surgical technician and also designed and arranged for the local production of medical equipment for the unit. He received a Medal of Honor with a bronze stallion and two gold stars from that country for his work.

Mr. Diggs has been featured on numerous radio and television shows including "To Tell The Truth" and "Oprah". He has been referenced in various books such as *The Hits Just Keep On Coming*: The History of Top 40 Radio, by Ben Fong-Torres; *Mark at Thirty*, A life making headlines by Alvin Guthertz, *South Dakota Curiosities* by Bernie Hunhoff, *South Dakota* by Michael Burgan, and *First Imagine* by John Miller.

Epilogue

It is my hope that this book will have raised some questions about the nature of reality that will stimulate some interesting conversations. There may be no answers to these questions, but the journey to finding answers could lead to some new and interesting experiences and ways of viewing your present location in time and space. They could also lead to bringing some new and interesting people into your life.

Be sure to consider some of the books in the suggested reading list. They offer a more in depth look into some of these ideas.

I created most of the artwork in this book originally in color. You can see many of these images in color on my art website www.DiggsArt.com where they can also be purchased.

Email me to get on my mailing list and connect with fellow travelers. I would be happy to bring an Interactive Animation Presentation to your living room, educational or religious institution or event. Contact me for details, me@ldiggs.com or check out the website at www.DiggsArt.com. Make sure you respond to the "robot generated spam control message" you will receive the first time you email me.

Suggested Reading

Dancing Wu Li Masters: An Overview of the New Physics by Gary Zukav

Willful Blindness by Margaret Heffernan

Brain Rules: 12 Principles for Surviving and Thriving at Work, Home, and School by John Medina

Future Babble: Why Expert Predictions Fail - and Why We Believe Them Anyway by Dan Gardner

Incognito: The Secret Lives of the Brain by David Eagleman

Fooled by Randomness: The Hidden Role of Chance in Life and in the Markets by Nassim Nicholas Taleb

The Head Trip: Adventures on the Wheel of Consciousness by Jeff Warren

The Hidden Reality: Parallel Universes and the Deep Laws of the Cosmos by Brian Greene

How We Decide by Jonah Lehrer

The Information: A History, A Theory, A Flood by James Gleick

Instant Egghead Guide: The Mind by Emily Anthes, Scientific American and Steve Mirsky

The Invisible Gorilla: And Other Ways Our Intuitions Deceive Us by Christopher Chabris

Predictably Irrational; The Hidden Forces That Shape Our Decisions by Dan Ariely

Irrationality: The Enemy Within by Stuart Sutherland, James Ball and Ben Goldacre

Mindless Eating: Why We Eat More Than We Think by Brian Wansink Ph.d.

Unseen Diversity: The World of Bacteria by Betsey Dexter Dyer

The Sociopath Next Door by Martha Stout Ph.D.

Subliminal Persuasion: Influence & Marketing Secrets They Don't Want You To Know by Dave Lakhani

Wherever You Go, There You Are: Mindfulness Meditation In Everyday Life by Jon Kabat-Zinn

Why We Make Mistakes: How We Look Without Seeing, Forget Things in Seconds, and Are All Pretty Sure We Are Way... by Joseph T Hallinan

13 Things That Don't Make Sense: The Most Baffling Scientific Mysteries of Our Time by Michael Brooks and James Adams

www.ingramcontent.com/pod-product-compliance
Lightning Source LLC
Chambersburg PA
CBHW071013040426
42443CB00007B/750